THE PHILLIP KEVEREN SERIES   PIANO SOLO

BILLY JOEL
FOR CLASSICAL PIANO

Cover Photo by Paul Natkin/Getty Images

— PIANO LEVEL —
ADVANCED

ISBN 978-1-4950-7034-1

HAL•LEONARD®
CORPORATION

7777 W. BLUEMOUND RD. P.O. BOX 13819 MILWAUKEE, WI 53213

In Australia Contact:
Hal Leonard Australia Pty. Ltd.
4 Lentara Court
Cheltenham, Victoria, 3192 Australia
Email: ausadmin@halleonard.com.au

Visit Hal Leonard Online at
www.halleonard.com

Visit Phillip at
www.phillipkeveren.com

PREFACE

In 1997, I had the privilege of working with Billy Joel to bring his pop tunes together with classical piano styles. The book that emerged from that collaboration, *Billy Joel Easy Classics*, was designed for the developing pianist. I arranged a second collection of advanced settings that, for a variety of administrative reasons, never made it to print at that time.

Fast forward to 2016: The pencil manuscripts of the aforementioned advanced arrangements were discovered in an abandoned file cabinet in Hal Leonard Corporation's offices in Milwaukee. So here they are, nearly 20 years later – arriving, at last, in the publication you are holding.

Billy Joel's songs are exquisite works of art, well suited in every way for classical piano treatments. The most difficult decision is deciding what shade of classical is best for the song – Baroque, Romantic, Impressionist, or...? I hope that, upon playing each piece, you will enjoy the musical journey.

Sincerely,

Phillip Keveren

BIOGRAPHY

Phillip Keveren, a multi-talented keyboard artist and composer, has composed original works in a variety of genres from piano solo to symphonic orchestra. Mr. Keveren gives frequent concerts and workshops for teachers and their students in the United States, Canada, Europe, and Asia. Mr. Keveren holds a B.M. in composition from California State University Northridge and a M.M. in composition from the University of Southern California.

CONTENTS

AND SO IT GOES

Words and Music by
BILLY JOEL
Arranged by Phillip Keveren

Rubato, with reflection (♩ = 50)

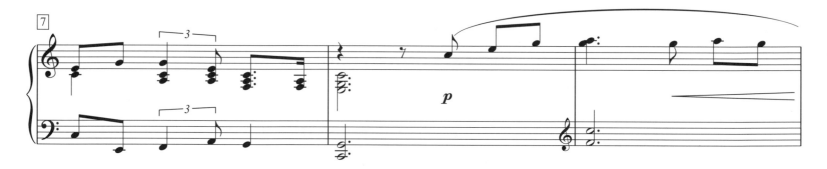

C'ETAIT TOI
(You Were the One)

Words and Music by
BILLY JOEL
Arranged by Phillip Keveren

HONESTY

Words and Music by
BILLY JOEL
Arranged by Phillip Keveren

Slowly, with deep expression (♩ = 58)

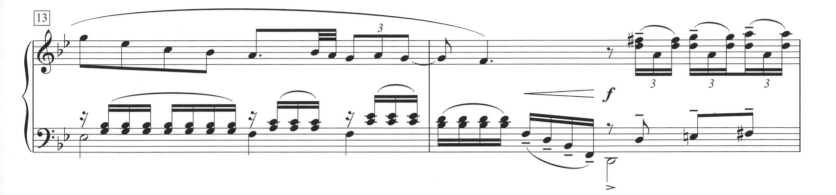

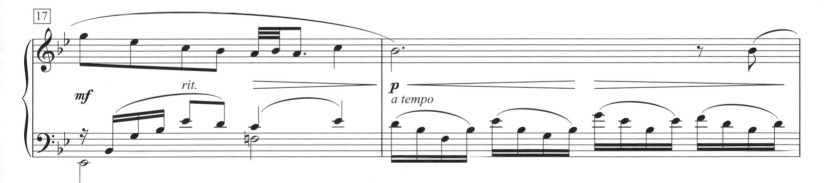

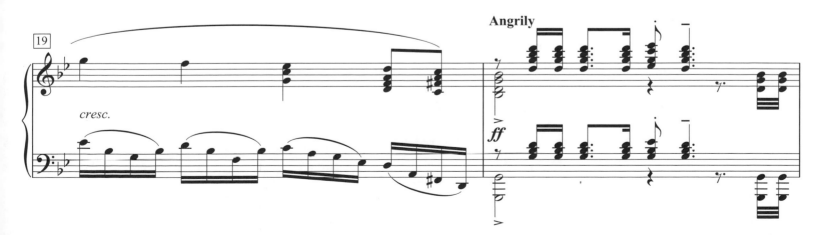

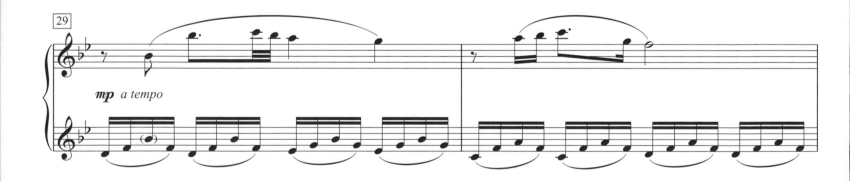

IF I ONLY HAD THE WORDS

(To Tell You)

Words and Music by
BILLY JOEL
Arranged by Phillip Keveren

With simple tenderness (♩ = 69)

With pedal

cantabile

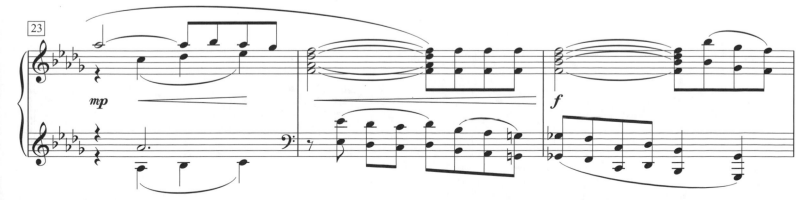

14

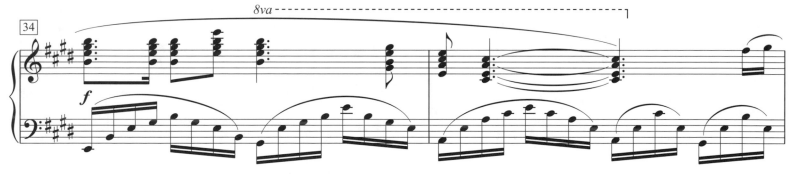

AN INNOCENT MAN

Words and Music by
BILLY JOEL
Arranged by Phillip Keveren

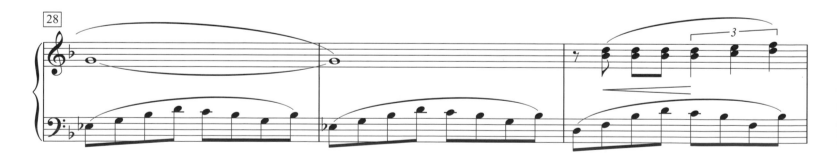

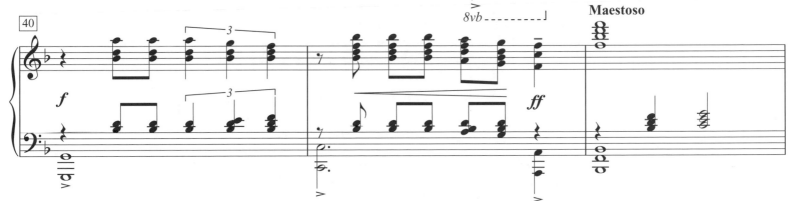

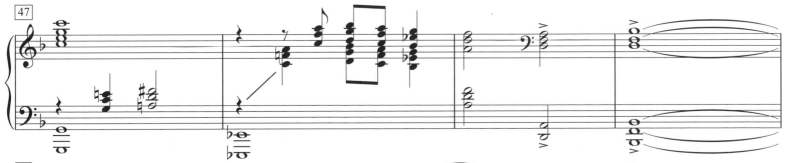

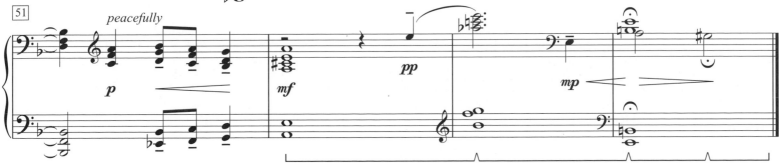

IT'S STILL ROCK AND ROLL TO ME

Words and Music by
BILLY JOEL
Arranged by Phillip Keveren

Brilliantly (♩. = 126)

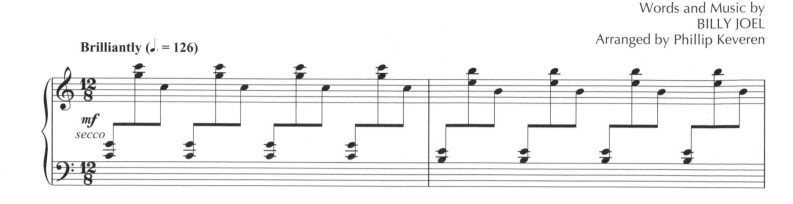

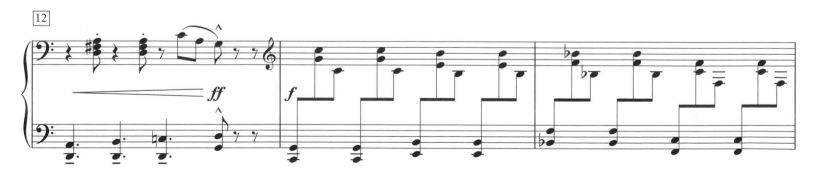

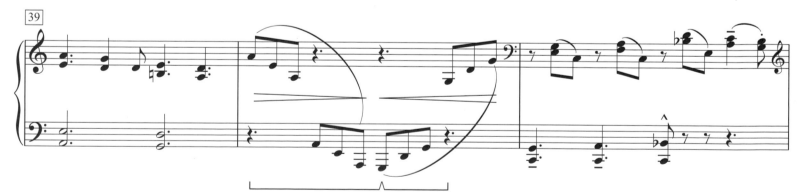

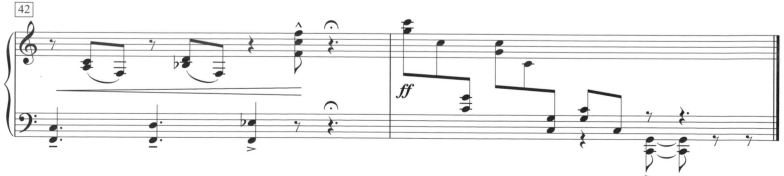

PIANO MAN

Words and Music by
BILLY JOEL
Arranged by Phillip Keveren

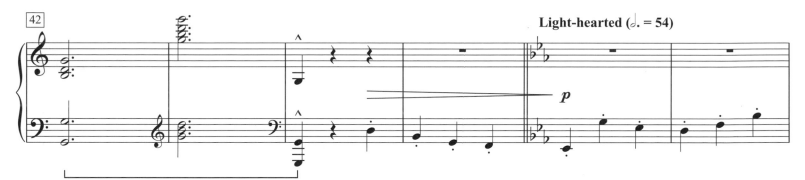

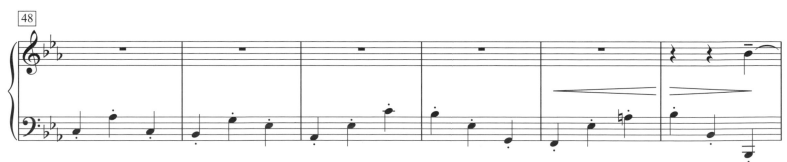

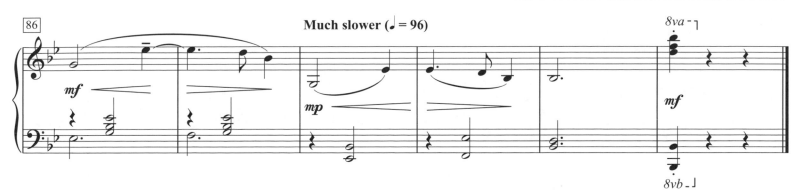

LENINGRAD

Words and Music by
BILLY JOEL
Arranged by Phillip Keveren

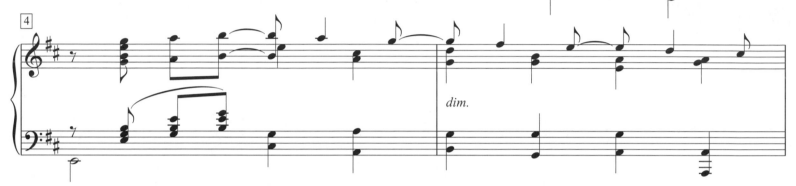

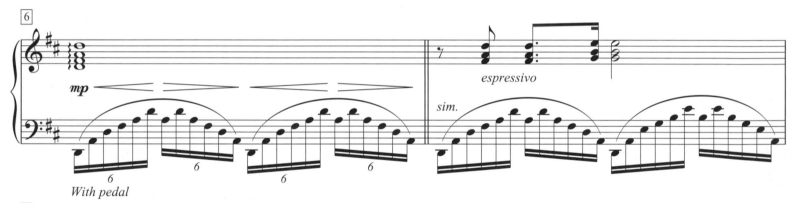

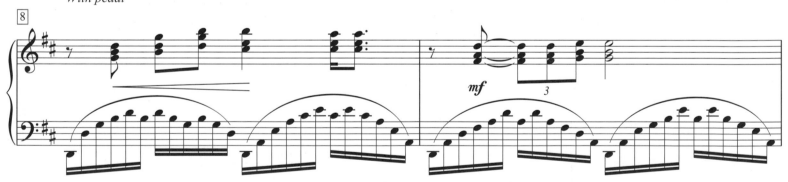

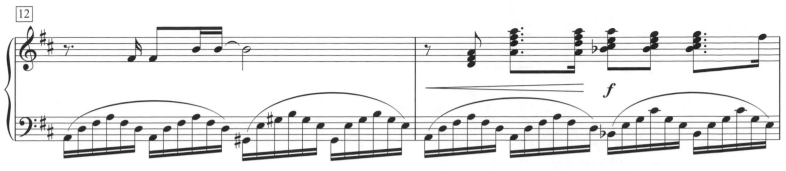

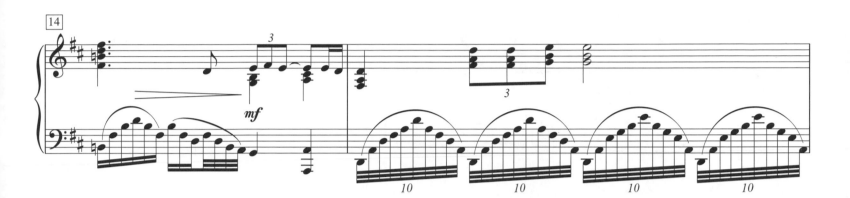

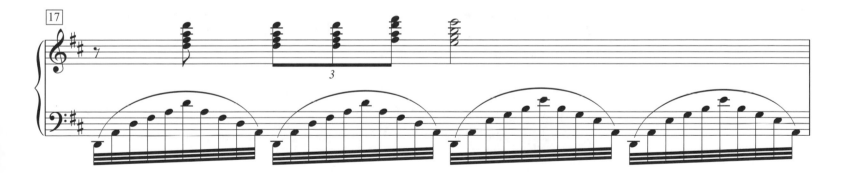

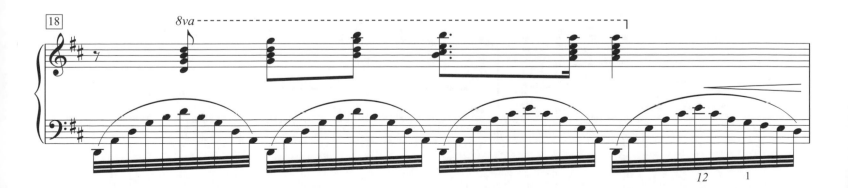

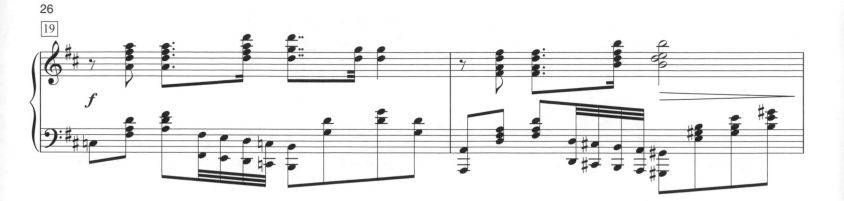

LULLABYE
(Goodnight, My Angel)

Words and Music by
BILLY JOEL
Arranged by Phillip Keveren

Rubato espressivo (♩ = 72)

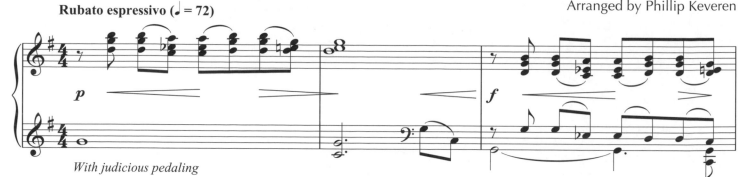

With judicious pedaling

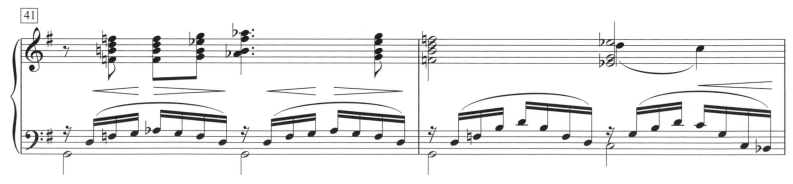

SHE'S ALWAYS A WOMAN

Words and Music by
BILLY JOEL
Arranged by Phillip Keveren

Andante con moto (♩. = 56)

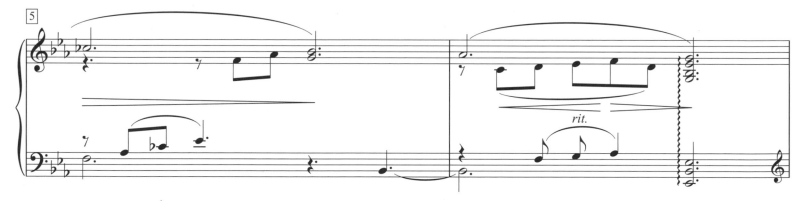

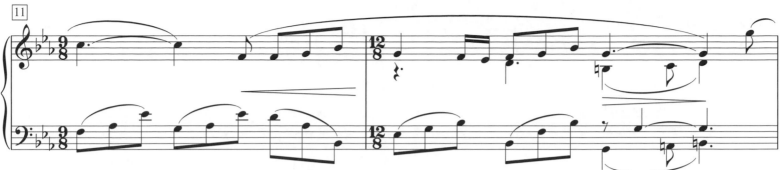

Cadenza (rubato)

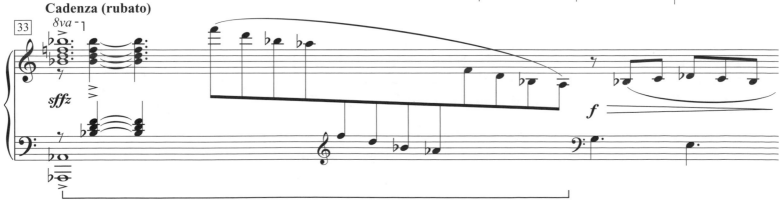

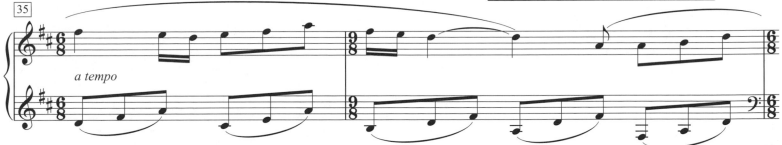

UPTOWN GIRL

Words and Music by
BILLY JOEL
Arranged by Phillip Keveren

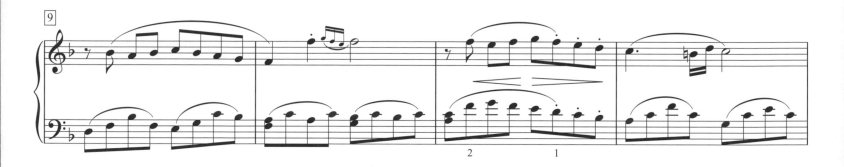

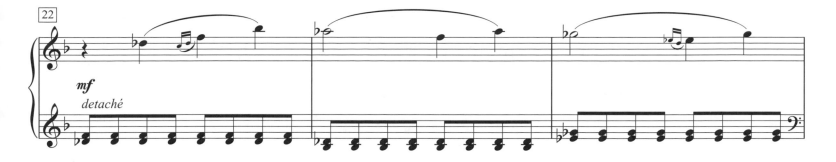

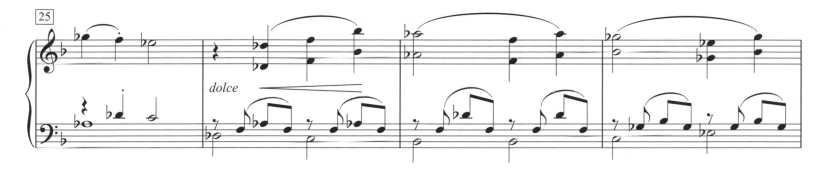

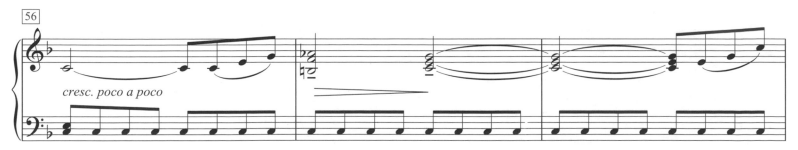

D.S. al Coda

CODA

THE PHILLIP KEVEREN SERIES

PIANO SOLO

00156644	**ABBA for Classical Piano**	$15.99
00311024	**Above All**	$12.99
00311348	**Americana**	$12.99
00198473	**Bach Meets Jazz**	$14.99
00313594	**Bacharach and David**	$15.99
00306412	**The Beatles**	$17.99
00312189	**The Beatles for Classical Piano**	$16.99
00275876	**The Beatles – Recital Suites**	$19.99
00312546	**Best Piano Solos**	$15.99
00156601	**Blessings**	$12.99
00198656	**Blues Classics**	$12.99
00284359	**Broadway Songs with a Classical Flair**	$14.99
00310669	**Broadway's Best**	$14.99
00312106	**Canzone Italiana**	$12.99
00280848	**Carpenters**	$16.99
00310629	**A Celtic Christmas**	$12.99
00310549	**The Celtic Collection**	$12.95
00280571	**Celtic Songs with a Classical Flair**	$12.99
00263362	**Charlie Brown Favorites**	$14.99
00312190	**Christmas at the Movies**	$14.99
00294754	**Christmas Carols with a Classical Flair**	$12.99
00311414	**Christmas Medleys**	$14.99
00236669	**Christmas Praise Hymns**	$12.99
00233788	**Christmas Songs for Classical Piano**	$12.99
00311769	**Christmas Worship Medleys**	$14.99
00310607	**Cinema Classics**	$15.99
00301857	**Circles**	$10.99
00311101	**Classic Wedding Songs**	$10.95
00311292	**Classical Folk**	$10.95
00311083	**Classical Jazz**	$12.95
00137779	**Coldplay for Classical Piano**	$16.99
00311103	**Contemporary Wedding Songs**	$12.99
00348788	**Country Songs with a Classical Flair**	$14.99
00249097	**Disney Recital Suites**	$17.99
00311754	**Disney Songs for Classical Piano**	$17.99
00241379	**Disney Songs for Ragtime Piano**	$17.99
00311881	**Favorite Wedding Songs**	$14.99
00315974	**Fiddlin' at the Piano**	$12.99
00311811	**The Film Score Collection**	$15.99
00269408	**Folksongs with a Classical Flair**	$12.99
00144353	**The Gershwin Collection**	$14.99
00233789	**Golden Scores**	$14.99
00144351	**Gospel Greats**	$12.99
00183566	**The Great American Songbook**	$12.99
00312084	**The Great Melodies**	$12.99
00311157	**Great Standards**	$12.95
00171621	**A Grown-Up Christmas List**	$12.99
00311071	**The Hymn Collection**	$12.99
00311349	**Hymn Medleys**	$12.99

00280705	**Hymns in a Celtic Style**	$12.99
00269407	**Hymns with a Classical Flair**	$12.99
00311249	**Hymns with a Touch of Jazz**	$12.99
00310905	**I Could Sing of Your Love Forever**	$12.95
00310762	**Jingle Jazz**	$14.99
00175310	**Billy Joel for Classical Piano**	$16.99
00126449	**Elton John for Classical Piano**	$16.99
00310839	**Let Freedom Ring!**	$12.99
00238988	**Andrew Lloyd Webber Piano Songbook**	$14.99
00313227	**Andrew Lloyd Webber Solos**	$15.99
00313523	**Mancini Magic**	$16.99
00312113	**More Disney Songs for Classical Piano**	$16.99
00311295	**Motown Hits**	$14.99
00300640	**Piano Calm**	$12.99
00339131	**Piano Calm: Christmas**	$12.99
00346009	**Piano Calm: Prayer**	$14.99
00306870	**Piazzolla Tangos**	$16.99
00156645	**Queen for Classical Piano**	$15.99
00310755	**Richard Rodgers Classics**	$16.99
00289545	**Scottish Songs**	$12.99
00310609	**Shout to the Lord!**	$14.99
00119403	**The Sound of Music**	$14.99
00311978	**The Spirituals Collection**	$10.99
00210445	**Star Wars**	$16.99
00224738	**Symphonic Hymns for Piano**	$14.99
00279673	**Tin Pan Alley**	$12.99
00312112	**Treasured Hymns for Classical Piano**	$14.99
00144926	**The Twelve Keys of Christmas**	$12.99
00278486	**The Who for Classical Piano**	$16.99
00294036	**Worship with a Touch of Jazz**	$12.99
00311911	**Yuletide Jazz**	$17.99

EASY PIANO

00210401	**Adele for Easy Classical Piano**	$15.99
00310610	**African-American Spirituals**	$10.99
00218244	**The Beatles for Easy Classical Piano**	$14.99
00218387	**Catchy Songs for Piano**	$12.99
00310973	**Celtic Dreams**	$12.99
00233686	**Christmas Carols for Easy Classical Piano**	$12.99
00311126	**Christmas Pops**	$14.99
00311548	**Classic Pop/Rock Hits**	$14.99
00310769	**A Classical Christmas**	$10.95
00310975	**Classical Movie Themes**	$12.99
00144352	**Disney Songs for Easy Classical Piano**	$12.99
00311093	**Early Rock 'n' Roll**	$14.99
00311997	**Easy Worship Medleys**	$12.99
00289547	**Duke Ellington**	$14.99
00160297	**Folksongs for Easy Classical Piano**	$12.99

00110374	**George Gershwin Classics**	$12.99
00310805	**Gospel Treasures**	$12.99
00306821	**Vince Guaraldi Collection**	$19.99
00160294	**Hymns for Easy Classical Piano**	$12.99
00310798	**Immortal Hymns**	$12.99
00311294	**Jazz Standards**	$12.99
00310744	**Love Songs**	$12.99
00233740	**The Most Beautiful Songs for Easy Classical Piano**	$12.99
00220036	**Pop Ballads**	$14.99
00311406	**Pop Gems of the 1950s**	$12.95
00311407	**Pop Gems of the 1960s**	$12.95
00233739	**Pop Standards for Easy Classical Piano**	$12.99
00102887	**A Ragtime Christmas**	$12.99
00311293	**Ragtime Classics**	$10.95
00312028	**Santa Swings**	$12.99
00233688	**Songs from Childhood for Easy Classical Piano**	$12.99
00103258	**Songs of Inspiration**	$12.99
00310840	**Sweet Land of Liberty**	$12.99
00126450	**10,000 Reasons**	$14.99
00310712	**Timeless Praise**	$12.95
00311086	**TV Themes**	$12.99
00310717	**21 Great Classics**	$12.99
00160076	**Waltzes & Polkas for Easy Classical Piano**	$12.99
00145342	**Weekly Worship**	$16.99

BIG-NOTE PIANO

00310838	**Children's Favorite Movie Songs**	$12.99
00346000	**Christmas Movie Magic**	$12.99
00277368	**Classical Favorites**	$12.99
00310907	**Contemporary Hits**	$12.99
00277370	**Disney Favorites**	$14.99
00310888	**Joy to the World**	$12.99
00310908	**The Nutcracker**	$12.99
00277371	**Star Wars**	$16.99

BEGINNING PIANO SOLOS

00311202	**Awesome God**	$12.99
00310837	**Christian Children's Favorites**	$12.99
00311117	**Christmas Traditions**	$10.99
00311250	**Easy Hymns**	$12.99
00102710	**Everlasting God**	$10.99
00311403	**Jazzy Tunes**	$10.95
00310822	**Kids' Favorites**	$12.99
00338175	**Silly Songs for Kids**	$9.99

PIANO DUET

00126452	**The Christmas Variations**	$12.99
00311350	**Classical Theme Duets**	$10.99
00295099	**Gospel Duets**	$12.99
00311544	**Hymn Duets**	$14.99
00311203	**Praise & Worship Duets**	$12.99
00294755	**Sacred Christmas Duets**	$12.99
00119405	**Star Wars**	$14.99
00253545	**Worship Songs for Two**	$12.99

Prices, contents, and availability subject to change without notice.
0221